What's in this book

This book belongs to

_____

请喝茶 At the Chinese restaurant

学习内容 Contents

沟通 Communication

称呼家庭成员
Address family members

请他人喝饮料
Offer someone a drink

表达疑问
Express doubt

生词 New words

★	我们	we, us
★	你们	you
★	他们 / 她们	they, them
★	爷爷	grandfather, grandpa
★	奶奶	grandmother, grandma
★	请	please
★	个	(measure word)
★	呢	(interrogative particle)

五月花

茶　　　　tea

说话　　　to speak

办法　　　idea, method

爷爷奶奶，请喝茶。
Grandma and Grandpa,
please have some tea.

怎么办呢？
What should I do?

文化 Cultures

中国孝的概念
Filial piety in Chinese culture

跨学科学习 Project

制作糖果相框，写中文节日卡
Make a photo frame using sweets
and write a card in Chinese

Get ready

1 Do you like going to Chinese restaurants?

2 Who do you like going with?

3 What do you do when you have meals with your family?

wǒ men
我们

星期日，我们和爷爷
奶奶一起上茶楼。

爸爸和爷爷看球，他们
不说话。

妈妈看手机、姐姐画画，
她们不说话。

没有人说话，也没有人
喝茶。奶奶不高兴。

怎么办呢？我有一个办法。

你们 nǐ men

请 qǐng

喝茶 hē chá

"爷爷奶奶，你们请喝茶。"我和姐姐说。

Let's think

1 Why is Grandma unhappy? Tick the boxes.

2 Look carefully. Circle the Chinese food.

New words

1 Learn the new words.

2 Complete the sentences. Write the letters.

a 我们　　b 你们　　c 他们　　d 她们　　e 爷爷　　f 奶奶

1 ＿＿ 喜欢唱歌。

2 ＿＿ 有一个足球。

3 ＿＿ 是我的 ＿＿ 和 ＿＿。

4 ＿＿ 请喝茶。

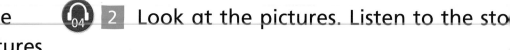
听听说说 Listen and say

🎧 03 **1** Listen and circle the correct pictures.

🎧 04 **2** Look at the pictures. Listen to the sto

1

2

3

① 爷爷奶奶，请喝茶。

③ 我有一个苹果。

我有两个苹果。

d say.

1

2

Task

Stick a picture of your grandparents in the space below. Tell your friends about them.

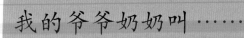

我的爷爷奶奶叫 ……

Paste your photo here.

我们一起玩。

我们一起画画。

Game

Point to the shapes and find out what your friend likes or does not like to do.

你喜欢踢足球吗？

喝茶

我喜欢踢足球。

踢足球

我喜欢唱歌，你呢？

和小狗玩

画画

吃水果

看书

我不喜欢唱歌，我喜欢和小狗玩。

唱歌

Song

爷爷奶奶，你们请喝茶。

爸爸妈妈，你们请吃水果。

哥哥姐姐，你们喝果汁吗？

弟弟妹妹，

你们和我一起玩吗？

课堂用语 Classroom language

玩游戏。
Play a game.

赢了。输了。
I won. I lost.

 Write

1 Learn and trace the stroke.

竖弯钩

2 Revise and trace the strokes.

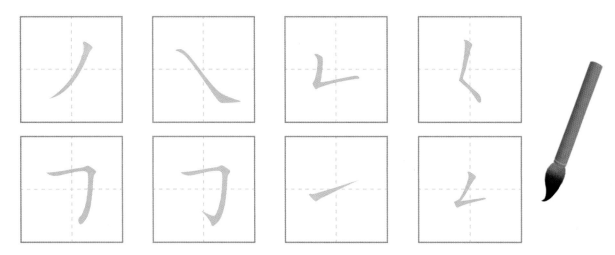

3 There are six components in the picture. Can you write them?

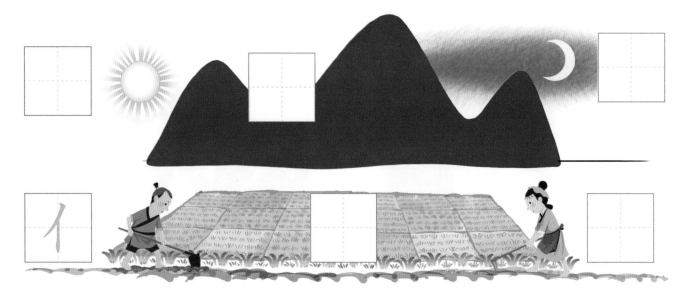

4 Trace and write the characters.

ノ イ 化 化 他

| 他 | 他 | | |

乙 夕 女 女 如 她

| 她 | 她 | | |

5 Write and say.

| | 们 |

| | 们 |

汉字小常识 Did you know?

When talking about more than one person, remember to use 们 .

Read the words aloud.

你
他
她
男孩
女孩
朋友

我

我们

你们
他们
她们
男孩们
女孩们
朋友们

Cultures

1 Do you know how Chinese people show respect for their elders?

孝

Filial piety means to be good to one's parents and the elders. It is very important in Chinese culture.

2 How do you show respect for your elders? Write on the note paper.

1 Would you like to give your parents a special photo frame? Follow the steps to make one.

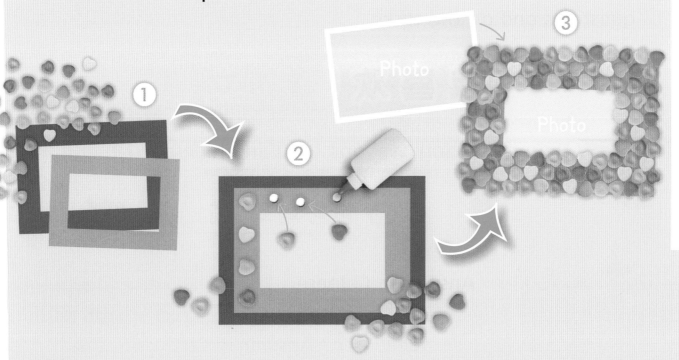

2 Make your grandparents a card. Draw their faces and colour the Chinese words.

爷爷 奶奶 我 爱 你们!

Grandpa & Grandma, I love you!

1 Read the messages in the fortune cookies. Answer the questions and do the tasks.

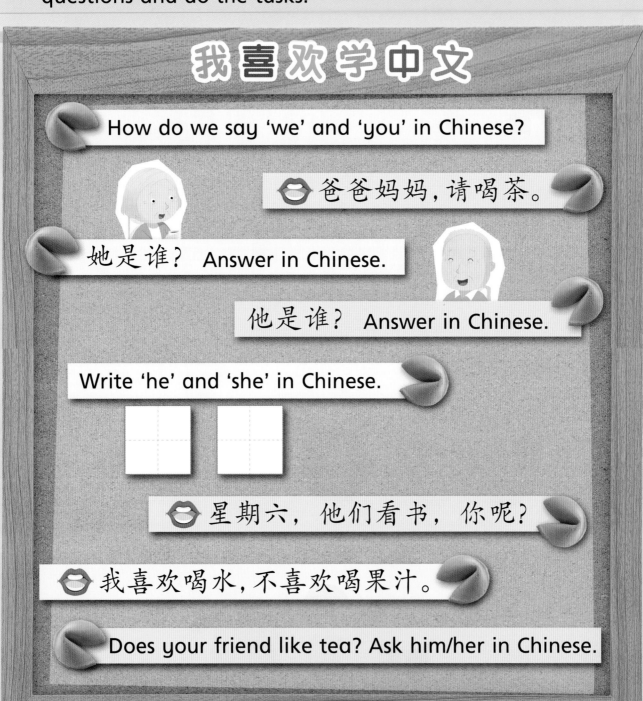

我喜欢学中文

How do we say 'we' and 'you' in Chinese?

爸爸妈妈，请喝茶。

她是谁？ Answer in Chinese.

他是谁？ Answer in Chinese.

Write 'he' and 'she' in Chinese.

星期六，他们看书，你呢？

我喜欢喝水，不喜欢喝果汁。

Does your friend like tea? Ask him/her in Chinese.

2 Work with your friend. Colour the stars and the chilies.

Words	说	读	写
我们	☆	☆	🌶
你们	☆	☆	🌶
他们	☆	☆	🌶
她们	☆	☆	🌶
爷爷	☆	☆	🌶
奶奶	☆	☆	🌶
请	☆	☆	🌶
个	☆	☆	🌶
呢	☆	☆	🌶

Words and sentences	说	读	写
茶	☆	🌶	🌶
说话	☆	🌶	🌶
办法	☆	🌶	🌶
爷爷奶奶，请喝茶。	☆	🌶	🌶
怎么办呢？	☆	🌶	🌶

Address family members	☆
Offer someone a drink	☆
Express doubt	☆

3 What does your teacher say?

My teacher says ...

分享 Sharing

Words I remember

我们	wǒ men	we, us
你们	nǐ men	you
他们/她们	tā men/ tā men	they, them
爷爷	yé ye	grandfather, grandpa
奶奶	nǎi nai	grandmother grandma
请	qǐng	please
个	gè	(measure w
呢	ne	(interrogativ particle)

茶	chá	tea
说话	shuō huà	to speak
办法	bàn fǎ	idea, method

Other words

上	shàng	to go to
茶楼	chá lóu	Chinese restaurant
手机	shǒu jī	cell phone
也	yě	also, too
高兴	gāo xìng	glad, happy

OXFORD

UNIVERSITY PRESS

Oxford University Press is a department of the University of Oxford.
It furthers the University's objective of excellence in research, scholarship,
and education by publishing worldwide. Oxford is a registered trade mark of
Oxford University Press in the UK and in certain other countries

Published in Hong Kong by
Oxford University Press (China) Limited
39th Floor, One Kowloon, 1 Wang Yuen Street, Kowloon Bay,
Hong Kong

Illustrated by Anne Lee and Wildman

Photographs for reproduction permitted by Dreamstime.com

China National Publications Import & Export (Group) Corporation is an authorized distributor of
Oxford Elementary Chinese.

Please contact content@cnpiec.com.cn or 86-10-65856782

ISBN: 978-0-19-942981-3

10 9 8 7 6 5 4 3 2